VALENCIA

Travel Guide 2023-2024

Unraveling the Treasures of Spain's Enchanting Mediterranean Gem

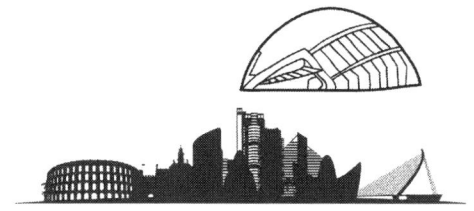

Alanna Marrow

Copyright © 2023 Alanna Marrow.

All rights reserved.

Thankful to you for consenting to protected innovation guidelines by downloading this book through genuine methods and by not replicating, checking, or spreading any piece of this book

Valencia Travel Guide 2023-2024

Table Of Contents

    Map Of Valencia
Introduction
Chapter One
    About Valencia
    History
    Culture
    Geography
Chapter Two
    Planning your trip to Valencia
    Budgeting (how to save money)
    When to visit
    How to get to Valencia
    Traveling Documents
    Local Costumes and Etiquettes of the people
    Languages spoken in Valencia
    Phrases for travel
Chapter Three
    Major Cities in Valencia
    Transportations
    Airports
    Taxi
    Car Rentals
    Railway Stations
Chapter Four
    Accommodations
    Resorts and Hotels
    Camping Sites
Chapter Five

Valencia Travel Guide 2023-2024

- Sightseeing
- Ancient Monuments
- Museums
- Shopping

Chapter Six
- Natural Beauty and Coastal Delights
- Valencia's Beautiful Beaches
- Gardens and Parks
- Albufera Natural Park Excursion

Chapter Seven
- Outdoor Adventures
- Hiking and Trekking Routes
- Water Sports and Activities

Chapter Eighth
- Food and Drinks
- Restaurants
- Local cuisine
- Local Drinks
- Street Foods

Chapter Nine
- Entertainment and Nightlife
- Pubs and bars

Chapter Ten
- Safety and Health
- Vaccinations
- Dealing with Emergencies

Conclusion

Map Of Valencia

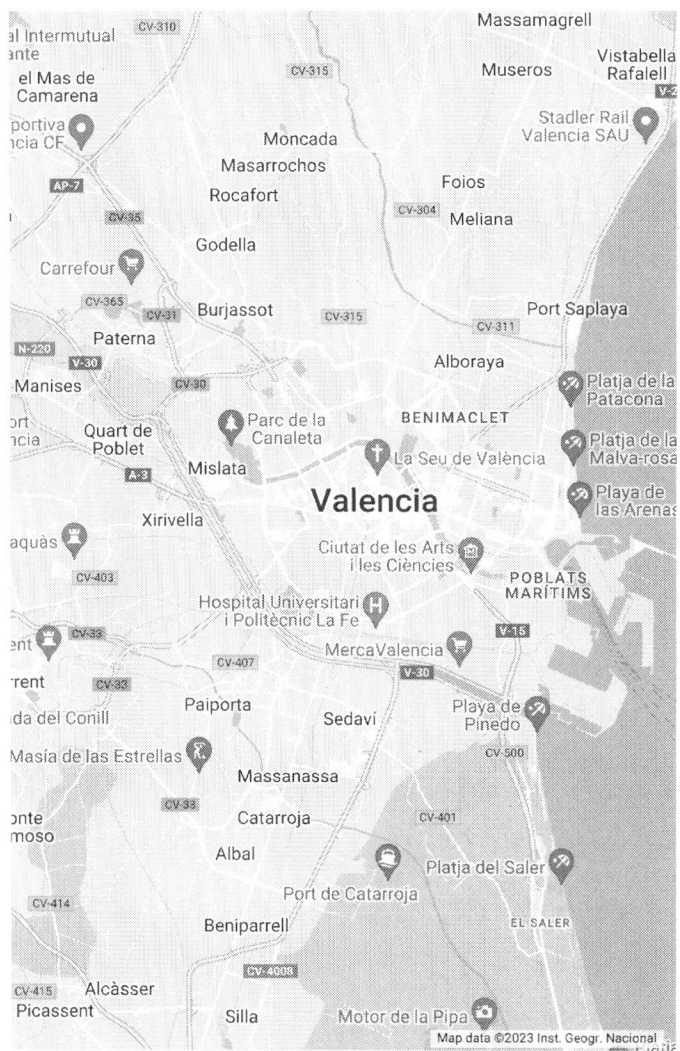

Introduction

Welcome to the "**Valencia Travel Guide 2023-2024**" - your key to unlocking the secrets of Spain's enchanting coastal gem! Nestled along the picturesque shores of the Mediterranean Sea, Valencia beckons travelers with its vibrant culture, rich history, and awe-inspiring landscapes. As you turn the pages of this comprehensive guide, we invite you to embark on a journey that promises to be both memorable and transformative.

Our goal is to serve as your trusted companion, revealing the hidden treasures and must-see wonders of this captivating region. Whether you're a history buff delving into the remnants of ancient civilizations, an art enthusiast seeking inspiration in world-class museums, or a food lover eager to savor the tantalizing flavors of Valencian cuisine, this guide caters to all your interests and desires.

The year 2023-2024 holds a special allure for Valencia, as the city gears up to celebrate its past, embrace its present, and carve a path towards an exciting future. You'll witness festivals that breathe life into age-old traditions, engage in immersive cultural experiences, and partake in sustainable initiatives that safeguard the region's natural beauty for generations to come.

Inside these pages, we've carefully curated the most up-to-date information, insider tips, and local insights to ensure you make the most of your time in Valencia. Whether you're a first-time visitor or a returning traveler, this guide promises to offer something new and inspiring at every turn.

Explore the heart of the city, where centuries-old architecture blends harmoniously with modern structures, creating a fascinating juxtaposition of old and new. Venture to the sun-kissed beaches that beckon relaxation and leisure, or discover the sprawling natural parks that hold a wealth of ecological wonders waiting to be explored.

Indulge in the tantalizing flavors of Valencia's cuisine, renowned for its paella and mouthwatering delicacies, as well as its bustling markets that brim with fresh produce and local artisanal crafts. Engage with the warm and hospitable locals, and let the spirit of the city capture your heart.

Beyond the well-trodden paths, we also take you on rewarding day trips to neighboring towns, each with its unique charm and character, showcasing the region's diversity and cultural richness.

Valencia Travel Guide 2023-2024

As you set forth on your Valencia adventure, we encourage you to immerse yourself fully in the experiences that await you. Embrace the traditions, soak in the colors, flavors, and sounds that surround you, and let the essence of Valencia seep into your soul.

So, with this travel guide in hand, let's embark on an unforgettable journey through the heart of Valencia, where every moment is an invitation to discover the allure of Spain's radiant coastal jewel. The year 2023-2024 promises to be an extraordinary chapter in Valencia's story, and you are now an integral part of it.

Buckle up, dear traveler, for an adventure of a lifetime awaits! Let the pages of this book be your gateway to the captivating world of Valencia.

Chapter One

About Valencia

History

The history of Valencia is a tapestry made of fascinating stories and several rich cultural threads. It was established as a colony in the Roman Empire and was given the name "Valentia Edetanorum." Over the ages, different civilizations put their stamp on the city, forming its distinct character.

Valencia flourished as a significant center for the arts, sciences, and trade during the Islamic era. Amazing architectural wonders were created during its heyday, notably the famous Silk Exchange (La Lonja de la Seda). But the start of Christian control came with King James I of Aragon's successful conquest of the city in the 13th century.

The subsequent centuries brought both prosperity and challenges, with wars and conflicts determining Valencia's future. Valencia's Renaissance period saw a flourishing of arts and literature, nurturing great minds like the renowned Valencian author Joanot Martorell, author of the chivalric romance "Tirant lo Blanch."

Valencia had tremendous industrialization and urban expansion in the 20th century. The stunning "Exposición Regional Valenciana" in 1909 and the universally recognized "Exposición Internacional" in 2000 marked the pinnacle of the transition.

Valencia is a thriving, international city today that values both tradition and progress. It continues to attract tourists from all over the world thanks to its history, which is reflected in its architecture, customs, and regional culture, making it a timeless destination where the past and present coexist together.

Culture

Valencian culture is centered on music and dancing. Traditional music from the area, such as the soul-stirring flamenco tunes, perfectly encapsulates its passionate nature. Parades, music, and fireworks fill the streets during celebrations like Las Fallas, illustrating the city's raucous revelry.

Another aspect of Valencian culture is art. The city is a mecca for artists, with everything from gorgeous Gothic and Renaissance architecture to contemporary avant-garde galleries. Masterpieces by renowned Valencian painters may be found in the Museu de Belles Arts, and cutting-edge architecture can be seen in the City of Arts and Sciences, a futuristic building.

Valencian culture is fundamentally based on its culinary delights. The city's trademark dish, paella, is well-known around the world, and residents are proud of their culinary heritage. Bustling marketplaces like Mercat Central offer a feast for the senses, luring foodies with fresh ingredients and regional delicacies.

The culture is strongly rooted in the ideals of the family and the community. Festivals, religious occasions, and social events give individuals the chance to join together, building links and a sense of belonging.

Geography

Valencia, located on Spain's scenic east coast, is a region blessed with a diversified and enthralling landscape. Its strategic location on the Mediterranean Sea's coast has had a significant impact on its history, culture, and economics.

About 518 kilometers of Valencia's breathtaking coastline are made up of numerous beaches that are popular with both visitors and locals. The coastal scenery can accommodate a variety of interests, whether it be relaxation or water sports, from the energetic metropolitan beaches like Malvarrosa and El Cabanyal to the serene coves and cliffs of the Costa Blanca.

Valencia's interior terrain is lush and fruitful as one travels further in. Large tracts of orange groves, olive groves, and vineyards cover the countryside in shades of green and gold in the Valencian Community, which is well known for its agriculture. The famous Valencian oranges are well known for their delectable sweetness.

Parks and natural reserves are abundant in the area. One such treasure is the Albufera Natural Park, a distinctive wetland ecosystem that supports conventional rice agriculture and offers crucial habitat for many bird species.

The magnificent Sierra Calderona and Sierra de Espadán mountain ranges can be found in Valencia's western region, in contrast to the coastal plains. These give guests the chance to go trekking and engage in other outdoor activities, rewarding them with spectacular views of the surroundings.

Valencia's topography has impacted its climate, making it a popular vacation spot all year round with moderate winters and pleasant summers.

Valencia's topography offers a varied playground for nature lovers and adventure seekers alike, whether they like to laze in the Mediterranean heat on sandy beaches, explore the picturesque wetlands, or head into the untamed mountains. The city's strong culture and history are well complemented by its beautiful landscapes and natural treasures, making it an alluring destination that satisfies the senses and the soul.

Chapter Two

Planning your trip to Valencia

Budgeting (how to save money)

Organizing a trip to Valencia can be thrilling, and by using some clever tactics, you can also save money as you go. Here are some suggestions to assist you in organizing an affordable trip to this fascinating city:

Flexible vacation Dates: Be flexible with your vacation dates and think about going in the spring or the autumn, which are considered to be the off-peak travel seasons for lodging and airfare.

Book Early: Plan and reserve your travel and lodging well in advance. This enables you to get better bargains and benefit from early bird discounts.

Select Affordable Accommodation: Look for inexpensive lodging options including hostels, guesthouses, or vacation rentals. These frequently offer relaxing stays for a small portion of the price of expensive hotels.

Use Valencia's effective and reasonably priced public transit system, which includes buses and trams, to navigate around the city. For unrestricted use of the public transit system and cheap entrance to attractions, think about getting a Valencia Tourist Card.

Take advantage of Valencia's numerous free and inexpensive attractions by strolling around the city's historic district, visiting parks and gardens, or relaxing on the beach.

Look for city passes or discount cards that provide discounts on attractions, museums, and public transportation. These can maximize your sightseeing while helping you save money.

Picnics and Local Markets: To enjoy reasonably priced, traditional Valencian food, choose picnics or local markets. Without spending a fortune, pick yourself some local delights and fresh veggies to enjoy.

Join free walking tours to learn about the city from professional guides. These tours frequently only accept tips, allowing you to pay what you can.

Travel by Foot or Bike: Walk or rent a bike to get about the city. Cycling can be a cheap and pleasurable method to find Valencia's hidden beauties because the city is walker-friendly.

Avoid Tourist Traps: Watch out for tourist traps that may impose exorbitant fees. Do some homework in advance to find authentic dining and shopping options that are fairly priced.

When to visit

Your choices for the weather, events, and crowd sizes will play a big role in determining the best time to visit Valencia. Here is a schedule to help you decide which season will provide the most memorable experiences for your trip:

Spring (March to May): Valencia blooms with vibrant flowers during the spring, making it a beautiful time to visit. The mild and pleasant weather is ideal for visiting outdoor sites and taking strolls along the beaches. Additionally, you can go to the well-known Las Fallas festival in March to see stunning sculptures and lively celebrations.

Summer (June to August): Valencia experiences a hot, sunny summer with the typical Mediterranean climate. The months of July and August, when many Europeans take their summer holidays, are the busiest travel months. Beaches and outdoor activities are booming, but be ready for bigger crowds and more expensive lodging.

Autumn (September to November): Autumn is a further fantastic season to visit Valencia. The temperature is still warm, but fewer people are visiting, making it easier for you to take advantage of the attractions. With a variety of wine and food events, the area marks the harvest season in October.

Winter (December to February): Valencia has mild winters, making it a good choice for those looking for a winter getaway. Although it can become colder, it doesn't often get below freezing. Wintertime travel means fewer tourists, quieter streets, and more affordable lodging. The city has a beautiful atmosphere in December thanks to the Christmas markets and festive decorations.

How to get to Valencia

By Air:

Valencia is served by Valencia Airport (VLC), which has excellent connections to significant Spanish and European cities. Valencia serves as a handy entry point for visitors from abroad thanks to the numerous airlines that run frequent flights to and from the city. Using the Aerobus shuttle or the Metrovalencia subway, you may quickly travel from the airport to the city center.

In a train:

Valencia is connected to important cities throughout Spain via high-speed and regional trains run by Renfe, Spain's national railway corporation. The high-speed AVE train provides a swift and comfortable journey whether you are coming from Madrid or Barcelona.

Valencia's primary train station, Estación del Norte, is conveniently situated and has excellent access to the city's public transport network.

By Bus:

Valencia is easily accessible from many Spanish cities because of the extensive bus network there, which includes ALSA and Avanza. The availability of international bus services from nearby nations makes them a practical choice for travelers on a tight budget.

By Car:

Driving to Valencia is a scenic and adaptable choice if you enjoy a road vacation. Major highways connect to the city, and the trip provides beautiful views of the Spanish countryside. However, keep in mind that parking in city centers can be few and pricey, so it's best to use the public transportation system or park-and-ride facilities.

Using a Cruise Ship:

Valencia's contemporary port is home to various cruise ships that greet passengers coming by sea. There's a good probability that your itinerary for a Mediterranean cruise may include the option to see the city.

Traveling Documents

Make sure your passport is valid for at least six months after the day you intend to depart Valencia. It is advised to renew your passport before your vacation if it is about to expire.

Check your country's requirements for a visa before traveling. For brief trips in Valencia (up to 90 days), citizens of the European Union (EU) and Schengen Area nations are normally not required to obtain a visa. But residents of other nations might need a Schengen visa. Make sure you apply for the necessary visa long before the dates of your trip.

Travel Insurance: Although not required, travel insurance is strongly advised to protect against unanticipated events like medical costs, trip cancellations, or lost luggage.

Flight Tickets: Reserve your airline tickets in advance for Valencia, and make sure you can easily access the printed or electronic versions while traveling.

Accommodation Confirmation: Keep copies of your reservations and confirmations handy for immigration requirements so you may give the address of your lodging.

Travel Schedule: Having a thorough travel schedule outlining your plans and activities while visiting Valencia is helpful. This may come in handy at immigration checks.

Driver's Licence (If Applicable): Bring your current driver's license if you intend to drive or hire a car in Valencia.

Depending on the laws in your native country, international driving licenses may also be necessary.

Bring a credit card that is accepted worldwide as well as some cash in euros for unforeseen needs like travel or little purchases.

Check if any vaccines are required or advised for travel to Valencia and bring the relevant immunization certificates.

Keep a list of emergency contacts on hand, including the Spanish consulate or embassy of your nation in case you require assistance while traveling.

Make copies or digital images of all necessary documents before your trip, and store them safely online or in a different piece of luggage. If something is lost or stolen, this precaution can be extremely helpful.

Local Costumes and Etiquettes of the people

Local Costumes:

1. Fallera/Fallero Attire: The Las Fallas festival is when the most recognizable Valencian costume is worn. The fallera costume is worn by women and consists of a fancy garment with detailed embroidery, a silk shawl, and jewelry. The male counterparts, known as falleros, dress traditionally in a white shirt, embroidered waistcoat (chaleco), and black trousers with a crimson necktie.

2. Traditional Dance Attire: Women participate in folklore dances while wearing colorful "gipsy" gowns with ruffled skirts and floral headpieces. Men dress in clothing like that of farmers, with wide-collared shirts, waist belts, and broad-brimmed hats.

Etiquette:

1. Greeting: A hard handshake is customary in Valencia when greeting a new acquaintance. Kisses on both cheeks are a common greeting between friends and strangers.

2. Respect for Elders: Valencians have high regard for seniors and address them by their first name after giving them formal titles like "Don" or "Doa".

3. Mealtime Customs: It is usual to wait until the host says "Bon profit" (enjoy your meal) before beginning to eat at meals. Additionally, it is considerate to eat everything on your plate rather than wasting any.

4. Dress code: Covering shoulders and knees is required when attending churches or other places of worship. Similarly to this, it is polite to dress appropriately when attending traditional events, especially during religious processions.

5. Siesta: Valencia, like many other Spanish cities, has a period in the afternoon when people take a nap. Plan because many stores and businesses can close for a few hours.

6. Punctuality: While being on time is appreciated in professional contexts, social gatherings sometimes start later, so being a little late is okay.

Languages spoken in Valencia

Valencia's linguistic diversity goes beyond Spanish, though, as the area also has two co-official tongues:

1. The Romance language of Valencia (**Valencià**) is different but closely linked to Catalan. The Valencian Community, which consists of the provinces of Valencia, Castellón, and Alicante, is co-official. In Valencia's local communities, Valencian is widely spoken and frequently utilized in governmental, media, and

educational contexts. Valencian is comparable to Catalan but also has its distinctive regional expressions.

2. The deaf and hard-of-hearing community in Valencia frequently uses **Spanish** Sign Language (Lengua de Signos Espanola, or LSE), a recognized sign language in Spain. LSE users must be able to access public services and institutions, hence sign language interpreters are a requirement.

In tourist regions, hotels, and restaurants in particular, English is also becoming more and more common. Many residents, especially the younger age, speak some English well and could be able to interact with tourists in simple English.

Phrases for travel

Useful Phrases for Travel in Valencia:

1. Greetings:

- Hello: ¡Hola! (OH-lah)

- Good morning: Buenos días (BWAY-nohs DEE-ahs)

- Good afternoon: Buenas tardes (BWAY-nahs TAR-dehs)

- Good evening/night: Buenas noches (BWAY-nahs NOH-ches)

- Goodbye: Adiós (ah-dee-OHS)

2. Polite Expressions:

- Please: Por favor (por fah-VOR)

- Thank you: Gracias (GRAH-see-ahs)

- You're welcome: De nada (deh NAH-dah)

- Excuse me / I'm sorry: Perdón / Lo siento (pehr-DON / loh SYEN-toh)

3. Basic Conversation:

- Yes: Sí (SEE)

- No: No (NO)

- How are you?: ¿Cómo estás? (KOH-moh ehss-TAHS?)

- I'm fine, thank you: Estoy bien, gracias (ehs-TOY byen, GRAH-see-ahs)

- What's your name?: ¿Cómo te llamas? (KOH-moh teh YAH-mahs?)

- My name is...: Me llamo... (meh YAH-moh...)

- Nice to meet you: Encantado/a de conocerte (en-kahn-TAH-doh/dah deh koh-noh-SEHR-teh)

4. Getting Around:

- Where is...?: ¿Dónde está...? (DOHN-deh ehs-TAH...?)

- How do I get to...?: ¿Cómo llego a...? (KOH-moh YEH-goh ah...?)

- Bus station: Estación de autobuses (ehs-tah-see-YON deh OW-toh-BOO-ses)

- Train station: Estación de tren (ehs-tah-see-YON deh tren)

- How much is the ticket?: ¿Cuánto cuesta el billete? (KWAHN-toh KWEHS-tah ehl bee-YEH-teh?)

5. Dining Out:

- Menu: Menú (meh-NOO)

- I would like...: Quisiera... (kee-SYEH-rah...)

- Water: Agua (AH-gwah)

- The bill, please: La cuenta, por favor (lah KWEN-tah, por fah-VOR)

6. Directions:

- Right: Derecha (deh-REH-chah)

- Left: Izquierda (eess-KYEHR-dah)

- Straight: Todo recto (TOH-doh REHK-toh)

- Street: Calle (KAH-yeh)

- Square: Plaza (PLAH-sah)

7. Emergencies:

- Help!: ¡Ayuda! (ah-YOO-dah!)

- I need a doctor: Necesito un médico (neh-seh-SEE-toh oon MEH-dee-koh)

- Police: Policía (poh-lee-SEE-ah)

- I'm lost: Estoy perdido/a (ehs-TOY pehr-DEE-doh/dah)

Remember, attempting to speak even a few basic phrases in the local language shows respect and often brings a smile to the faces of locals. Embrace the opportunity to connect with the people of Valencia and enhance your travel experience in this radiant coastal gem of Spain.

Chapter Three

Major Cities in Valencia

1. Valencia (València): Valencia, the region's main city and largest metropolitan center, is a bustling city renowned for its blend of modernity and historical riches. A few of its must-see attractions include the cutting-edge City of Arts and Sciences, the lovely Turia Gardens, and the well-known Central Market. The spectacular Las Fallas festival, which takes place in the city every year, is another thing that makes it famous.

2. Alicante (Alacant) is a coastal treasure on the Costa Blanca noted for its stunning beaches, exciting nightlife, and extensive cultural history. Spectacular views of the Mediterranean Sea may be found from the Castle of Santa Barbara, which stands watch over the city. Explanada de Espaa is a beautiful palm-lined

promenade where you may stroll while indulging in fresh seafood from the lively Mercado Central.

3. Castellón de la Plana is a city in northern Valencia that is well-known for its extensive sandy beaches and historical sites. Visit important locations like the Central Market, the Santa Maria Cathedral, and the Fadr bell tower. Natural parks surround the city, providing areas for exploration and outdoor recreation.

4. Elche (Elx): This city exemplifies the blending of nature and history with its enormous palm trees and UNESCO-listed Palm Grove of Elche. Visit the Basilica of Santa Maria, where the renowned "Misteri d'Elx" performance is presented, and explore the Elche Palmeral Museum.

5. Gandia: This coastal city is home to stunning beaches and significant maritime history. Playa de Gandia, one of the most well-liked beaches

in the area, is a great place to unwind after exploring the old Gandia Ducal Palace.

6. Sagunto (Sagunt) is well-known for its Roman and Moorish ruins, which include the magnificent Sagunto Castle and Roman Theatre. The city's old town is a labyrinth of little lanes that provides a window into its historic past.

Transportations

1. Metro and tram: The Metrovalencia system is a network of metro and tram lines that connects different areas of the city and reaches out to other cities. It's a great alternative for quick and inexpensive travel, especially when going to well-known tourist destinations like the City of Arts and Sciences or the coastal regions.

2. Bus: The EMT (Empresa Municipal de Transportes de València) operates a comprehensive bus network in Valencia. Buses

run throughout the entire city, giving visitors access to both the downtown and outlying areas. The Valencia Tourist Card is an affordable option for visitors because it provides unlimited trips on buses, the metro, and trams.

3. Bicycle: With a lot of bike lanes and rental options, Valencia is a bike-friendly city. Cycling is a fun way to take your time and explore the city. You may pick up and drop off bikes through the Valenbisi bike-sharing program at several locations around the city.

4. Walking: A lot of Valencia's attractions are close to one another, especially in the old city center. You can find attractive squares, shops, and alleys by exploring on foot.

5. Taxis: Taxis are easily accessible in Valencia and are a practical solution for traveling at odd hours or to specific locations. Make sure the

taxi's meter is running at all times, and get a receipt when you reach your destination.

6. Renting a car can be useful for day visits to adjacent towns and attractions, even though it is not necessary for seeing Valencia itself. There are car rental companies all across the city, including at the airport.

7. Train: The Renfe train network offers high-speed and regional train services for lengthier journeys to other Spanish cities. The primary train station in Valencia is Estación del Norte, which is conveniently situated and well-connected.

Airports

Valencia Airport (VLC), commonly known as Manises Airport, is the only airport that serves Valencia and is situated about 8 kilometers (km) west of the city center. Valencia Airport, one of Spain's busiest airports, serves as a convenient entry point for travelers from all over the world by connecting the area to many national and international destinations.

Services and Facilities:

A variety of amenities and services are available at Valencia Airport to make travel easy and comfortable. These consist of:

1. Terminals: A single terminal building at the airport houses both domestic and international flight operations. Modern amenities and a well-designed layout characterize the terminal.

2. Shops and Restaurants: There are several businesses, including duty-free shops, that offer a selection of trinkets, outfits, and other travel necessities to passengers. For meals and refreshments, there are numerous cafes, bars, and restaurants.

3. Transportation: The city center and adjacent areas are easily accessible from the airport. Public transit, taxis, or vehicle rental services

that are available at the airport make it simple for travelers to get where they're going.

4. Wi-Fi and connectivity: The terminal offers free Wi-Fi, enabling users to stay connected while traveling.

5. Lounges: Valencia Airport offers cozy lounges for passengers seeking a more tranquil and laid-back atmosphere while awaiting their flights. Some lounges also provide extra services like business centers and showers.

6. Accessibility: The airport is set up to accommodate travelers with disabilities or limited mobility, and special support services are offered upon request.

Airlines and Destinations:

Numerous airlines fly through Valencia Airport, which connects the area to many locations. Ryanair, Vueling, Iberia, Air Europa, and more well-known airlines fly out of the airport.

While popular international routes connect Valencia to locations throughout Europe and beyond, popular local routes connect Valencia to towns like Madrid, Barcelona, and Palma de Mallorca.

Transport to the City Center:

There are numerous ways for travelers to go from Valencia Airport to the city center. The Metrovalencia metro line offers a rapid and affordable trip from the airport to the city center and other Valencian areas. The Aerobus shuttle service also provides direct links from the airport to Plaza de Espaa, the city's central center. Those who prefer private transportation have access to taxis and automobile rental services.

Taxi

Services and Availability for Taxis:

Valencia has a constant supply of taxis that may be called on the street, found at designated taxi stands, or reserved via phone apps or hotel front desks. For convenient access, passengers can find taxi booths in well-traveled areas including transportation hubs, significant squares, and tourist sites.

Payment and Fares:

Valencia's taxi fares are controlled and adhere to a set scale of rates. The fare consists of a basic fee (referred to as the "bajada de bandera") and additional fees determined by the amount of time spent waiting and the distance traveled. To calculate the fare correctly, it is imperative to make sure the taxi meter is running from the start of the trip.

Although many cabs also take credit cards, most passengers pay for their taxi rides in cash. However, if you intend to pay with a card, it's usually a good idea to ask the driver first.

Communication through Language:

Although some taxi drivers in Valencia may be able to communicate in simple English, it's advisable to have your final location noted down or visible on a map to avoid any communication difficulties. For easier interactions with drivers, it can be helpful to know a few basic Spanish phrases.

Tipping:

Valencia does not require tips, however, it is traditional to round up the fare as a sign of gratitude for excellent service. A small tip is typically accepted if the driver offers great service or assists with luggage.

Accessibility:

Taxis in Valencia are designed to carry clients with special needs or limited mobility. On request, some taxi companies may also provide modified vehicles, but it is advised to make reservations in advance for such services.

Regulations and security:

To protect passenger safety, taxis in Valencia are driven by licensed drivers and are subject to tight restrictions. Inside the car, authorized taxis display their identification and registration details. To avoid any potential problems, it is advised to only hire authorized cabs.

Car Rentals

Companies that rent cars:

Valencia is home to numerous automobile rental agencies that provide a range of vehicle types to accommodate various needs and party sizes. At Valencia Airport and around the city, there are offices for both significant global brands and regional service providers.

Reservations and prerequisites:

It's simple to reserve a rental car in Valencia; you may do it online in advance, on arrival at the airport, or at several city locations. A valid driver's license, passport, and credit card for the security deposit are normally required to rent a car.

Various Vehicle Types

Valencia offers a wide selection of car rental options, from affordable models to high-end SUVs and minibusses for big parties. Consider elements like the number of passengers, luggage capacity, and the routes you plan to travel when selecting a car that suits your demands and budget.

Driving in Valencia:

Valencia has well-kept roads and clear signs, making driving relatively simple. It's important to be knowledgeable about the local traffic laws, though. All passengers are required to wear seat belts and speed limits are rigidly enforced. Unless you have a hands-free device, it is illegal to use a mobile phone while driving.

Parking:

Valencia provides both paid parking facilities (garages) and street parking. Parking may be scarce in the city's center, and certain locations are only accessible to locals. To prevent parking issues, it is advised to use public transport or park-and-ride locations when exploring the city.

Day Trips and Exploring Beyond Valencia:

Having a car rental in Valencia makes it possible to take exhilarating day trips to surrounding locations. With simplicity, visit the charming towns of Albufera National Park, relax in the hot springs of Montanejos, or travel to the ancient city of Sagunto. You may explore the many scenery and attractions of Valencia's surroundings at your own pace if you have a rental car.

Fuel and Toll Roads:

All across the city and on the main highways, there are several petrol stations. You should be aware that some of Spain's motorways contain tolls, so you should always have enough cash or credit cards on hand.

Railway Stations

1. Estación del Norte (North Station) is Valencia's primary train station and is housed in an opulent, historic structure in the middle of the city. It acts as a key center for both local and long-distance transportation, linking Valencia to locations throughout Spain, such as Madrid,

Barcelona, Alicante, and beyond. The station is a well-known icon in the city thanks to its appealing architectural features and striking façade.

2. Valencia's Joaqun Sorolla Station, also known as Joaqun Sorolla, is primarily used by Renfe's AVE high-speed trains. It has direct links to Madrid, Cuenca, and other locations along the high-speed rail network and is situated a little south of the city center. For those looking for effective rail connections, Joaqun Sorolla Station offers a contemporary and practical travel experience.

3. Estación de Valencia-Cabanyal (Cabanyal Station): Close to Valencia's seaside area, Cabanyal Station is a stop for regional Cercanas trains that connect to the city's many neighborhoods and municipalities. Travelers who want to tour the coastal regions or get to

Valencia's well-known beaches should stop at this station.

4. Several other Cercanas train stations, including Estación de Valencia-Sant Isidre, Estación de Valencia-San Vicente Martir, and Estación de Valencia-Fuente de San Luis, among others, also provide service to Valencia. These stations make it easy to move throughout the city and its environs.

Services and Facilities:

The passenger experience is improved by a variety of amenities and services available at Valencia's train stations. These consist of the following: ticket booths, automatic ticket machines, waiting areas, luggage storage, bathrooms, and stores. Additionally, some stations offer accessible amenities to help travelers with limited mobility.

Transfers and Connections:

With excellent connections to buses and the metro, Valencia's train stations make it simple for passengers to change to another form of transport and continue their excursions inside the city. In addition, taxis are easily accessible outside the stations for individuals who want to go privately.

Reservations & Ticketing:

You can buy train tickets at the stations' ticket windows, through automated machines, online through the Renfe website, or on other legitimate websites. It is advised to make reservations in advance, particularly for long-distance and AVE trains.

Chapter Four

Accommodations

Resorts and Hotels

1. Luxury lodging

Several luxurious hotels in Valencia offer first-rate facilities and services. These upscale hotels frequently provide spa services, fine dining restaurants, rooftop patios with spectacular city or ocean views, and attractive rooms with all the latest conveniences. With their convenient access to the city's cultural treasures, several luxury hotels are placed near popular sites.

2. Beachfront Hotels

Valencia provides an outstanding assortment of beachfront resorts along its scenic coastline for travelers looking for a beach vacation. These destinations offer easy access to the

Mediterranean Sea's blue waters and sandy beaches. The resort offers a variety of recreational opportunities for guests, including swimming, sunbathing, and participating in water sports, making it the ideal beach getaway.

3. Boutique lodging:

Valencia's boutique hotels provide a distinctive and individualized experience, whether housed in attractive old structures or chic new construction. With careful attention to detail in their décor and attentive service, these small resorts exhibit their unique character. Boutique hotels are frequently found in the center of the city, allowing visitors to fully experience Valencia's dynamic culture and atmosphere.

4. Affordable Accommodations:

Budget hotels and hostels, as well as other economical lodging choices, can be found in Valencia. These lodgings offer tidy, comfortable rooms, frequently with common bathrooms, making them a great option for budget-conscious travelers and backpackers.

5. Paradores:

Valencia is home to some incredible Paradores, which are distinctive hotels frequently located in old buildings like monasteries, castles, and palaces. These Paradores provide visitors the chance to fully experience Spain's illustrious past by fusing historical charm with contemporary convenience.

6. Hotels in City Centre:

The city's famous attractions, commercial areas, and vibrant dining scenes are all easily accessible to guests staying in Valencia's city center. For visitors eager to discover the city's cultural assets, many hotels in the city center offer convenience and character.

7. Resorts that welcome families:

Families are welcome in Valencia, which has a variety of family-friendly resorts that provide roomy lodging, kid-focused activities, and recreational amenities for all ages. These resorts offer the ideal location for a special family trip to the city or the beach.

Camping Sites

1. Camping near the beach:

Camping on the beach is a popular activity in Valencia thanks to its coastal setting. Many campgrounds along the breathtaking coastline provide easy access to sandy beaches and pristine waterways. Enjoy spectacular sunsets, wake up to the sound of the waves, and partake in a variety of water sports like swimming, snorkeling, and beach volleyball.

2. Nature Retreats:

Explore the gorgeous countryside to find campgrounds tucked away in the beauty of nature. These camping areas offer a peaceful and serene atmosphere because they are surrounded by verdant forests, undulating hills, or picturesque valleys. Hiking, birdwatching, or simply relaxing in a tranquil environment are all options.

3. Mountain Camping:

Valencia's interior has excellent mountain camping alternatives for outdoor enthusiasts. The Sierra Calderona, Sierra de Mariola, or Sierra de Espadán mountain ranges are stunning places to set camp. You can camp in the mountains to avoid the summer heat and take advantage of the cooler weather and stunning panoramic views.

4. Rural Camping:

In the charming villages of Valencia, find rural camping areas to get away from the noise and bustle of the metropolis. Interact with welcoming locals, take in the genuine charm of the Spanish countryside, and enjoy regional food. Camping in the country offers a chance to escape contemporary life and rediscover simpler pleasures.

5. Campsite Facilities:

The camping areas in Valencia are well-equipped with all the amenities needed for a comfortable stay. Most campgrounds offer spots for campervans and trailers as well as camping plots for tents. Clean restrooms and showers, electrical hookups, and water supply points are usual amenities. Additionally, some campgrounds could have Wi-Fi, shared kitchens, and laundry facilities.

6. Recreational Activities:

Camping in Valencia is an opportunity to embrace adventure as well as relaxation. Numerous campgrounds offer organized recreational activities like horseback riding, cycling, and nature walks. Camping is a fantastic family-friendly alternative because kids may play on playgrounds and participate in kids' groups.

7. Reservations and Regulations:

It's a good idea to reserve camping spots in advance, particularly during busy tourist times. Additionally, become familiar with the rules and regulations for camping at the particular location you select, such as any restrictions on campfires and how to dispose of waste.

Chapter Five

Sightseeing

Ancient Monuments

1. Roman Theater of Sagunto: is a remarkable reminder of the Roman presence in the region. It is found in the town of Sagunto, which is close to Valencia. The theatre, which had a seating capacity for thousands of people, was built in the first century BC, and its stunning remains today still display its magnificence.

2. Valencia Cathedral (Catedral de Santa Mara de Valencia): This magnificent cathedral is a fusion of Romanesque, Gothic, and Baroque architectural styles. It stands where a mosque once stood, and construction on it started in the 13th century. While the Holy Grail Chapel is thought to house the actual Holy Grail, the

Miguelete Tower provides sweeping views of the city.

3. Torres de Serranos: The Serranos Towers are a well-known representation of Valencia in the Middle Ages. The 14th century saw the main entry to the city being these imposing Gothic gates, which were previously a part of the city's old walls. They still exist as well-preserved historical monuments and provide sweeping vistas from the top.

4. Llotja de la Seda (Silk Exchange) is a Gothic architectural marvel and a key representation of Valencia's affluence in the 15th century. It is a UNESCO World Heritage Site. This magnificent structure, which once served as a hub for the commerce of silk, has a breathtaking main hall and superb workmanship.

5. Castle of Xàtiva: The Castle of Xàtiva is a powerful fortification with ancient origins dating back to the Iberian and Roman eras.

It is situated on a hill overlooking the town of Xàtiva. It served as a key location at various points in history and was later fortified by both Christians and Moors. Today, tourists are welcome to explore the ruin's remains and take in the stunning surroundings.

6. Almudín de Valencia: This grain storage facility from the Middle Ages dates to the 14th century. Almudn is a magnificent example of Valencian civic Gothic architecture with its massive front and lovely Gothic arches.

Museums

1. The City of Arts and Sciences (Ciudad de las Artes y las Ciencias) is an architectural wonder and a center for interdisciplinary research. There are several outstanding museums there:

The Principe Felipe Science Museum is an interesting, engaging, and educational science museum. It has interactive exhibits that cover diverse scientific theories and cutting-edge technology.

The Oceanogràfic is the biggest aquarium in Europe and features a staggering array of marine life in diverse water habitats. Visitors can interact with dolphins, belugas, and other marine animals while viewing mesmerizing underwater exhibits.

The Hemisfèric is a striking planetarium and IMAX theatre that provides immersive experiences on its enormous curved screen.

2. The Valencia Institute of Modern Art (Instituto Valenciano de Arte Moderno, or IVAM) is a renowned museum of contemporary art with a significant collection of modern and avant-garde works. It provides a wide variety of cultural events, art installations, and temporary exhibitions.

3. The Fine Arts Museum, also known as the Museo de Bellas Artes, is located in a magnificent 17th-century palace and features artwork from the Middle Ages to the 20th century. Famous Spanish artists such as Velázquez, Goya, and Sorolla have pieces in the collection.

4. Step back in time to experience Valencia's history, from its Roman antecedents to the current day, at the Valencia History Museum (Museo de Historia de Valencia). The museum offers a thorough overview of the city's past through the display of archaeological artifacts, historical records, and multimedia exhibits.

5. National Ceramics Museum (Museo Nacional de Cerámica): The magnificent Palace of the Marques de Dos Aguas is home to the National Ceramics Museum (Museo Nacional de Cerámica), which displays a magnificent collection of ceramics and ornamental arts. It

provides information about the traditional handicraft and aesthetic legacy of the area.

6. The Fallas Museum (Museo Fallero): Valencia is home to the renowned Las Fallas festival, which honors the creation of intricate sculptures. Some of the finest fallas (huge sculptures) from previous festivals are preserved by the Fallas Museum, providing a window into this distinctive cultural occasion.

7. Valencia's natural history, including geology, botany, and zoology, is displayed in the Natural Science Museum (Museu de les Ciències Naturals), which is situated in the city's old center. It has a sizable collection of taxidermied animals, minerals, and fossils.

Shopping

One of the must-visit shopping destinations in Valencia is the Central Market, a bustling haven for foodies. This impressive Art Nouveau building is a treasure trove of fresh produce, meats, and regional specialties. Strolling through its colorful stalls, you'll discover the essence of Valencian gastronomy.

For fashion enthusiasts, the Colón Market is a paradise. This beautifully restored market houses chic boutiques and designer stores, perfect for indulging in the latest trends. Meanwhile, Ruzafa, the city's hip neighborhood, is dotted with quirky shops, vintage stores, and independent designers, offering unique finds and one-of-a-kind pieces.

If you prefer the convenience of modern malls, head to Aqua Multiespacio or El Saler, where international brands and entertainment options await. And for artisanal crafts and souvenirs, the quaint streets surrounding Valencia Cathedral offer an authentic shopping experience.

Chapter Six

Natural Beauty and Coastal Delights

Valencia's Beautiful Beaches

1. One of Valencia's most well-known and recognizable beaches, Playa de la Malvarrosa, has a bustling scene with a mix of locals and tourists. Due to its expansive shoreline, beachgoers have plenty of room to enjoy beach activities like sunbathing. The promenade along the beach is lined with a variety of eateries and cafes that serve delectable paella and energizing drinks.

2. Playa de las Arenas: Playa de las Arenas is a neighboring beach to Playa de la Malvarrosa and is a charming area with a laid-back vibe that draws tourists. Families and individuals seeking a more calm environment like this beach.

Playa de las Arenas guarantees top-notch amenities and security for all beach lovers thanks to its Blue Flag designation.

3. Playa de El Saler: Located in the Albufera Natural Park, Playa de El Saler provides a more secluded beach experience. This beach, which is surrounded by dunes and pine forests, is a haven for nature enthusiasts and offers a tranquil respite from the bustle of the city.

4. Playa de la Patacona: This lovely beach is a local favorite and is located a little outside the city limits. It's the perfect place to relax and take in a serene day by the sea thanks to its calm waves and laid-back environment.

5. Playa de Port Saplaya, also referred to as "Little Venice," is a distinctive beach surrounded by charming pastel-colored homes and canals. This picturesque location fosters a romantic atmosphere, making it a well-liked vacation spot for couples.

Gardens and Parks

1. One of the city's most recognizable parks is Turia Gardens (Jardines del Turia), which was created when a disused riverbed was converted into a sizable green area. This linear park, which is nearly nine km long, features several leisure areas, playgrounds, fountains, and walking and cycling trails. A well-liked location for strolls, picnics, and outdoor activities is Turia Gardens.

2. The Royal Gardens, also known as Jardines del Real, is a tranquil and romantic setting close to Valencia's Royal Palace. These stunning gardens have several plant varieties, well-designed walks, and attractive fountains. While observing the architectural features of the garden, visitors can take in the peace.

3. The Monforte Gardens (Jardines de Monforte) is a lovely fusion of neoclassical and romantic styles and a little-known treasure in

Valencia. This garden exudes whimsy with its tier-set terraces, ornamental statuary, and water elements. It's the perfect place for a stroll or a quiet moment in the middle of nature.

4. Cabecera Park (Parque de Cabecera) is a wonderful family destination that is close to Valencia's Bioparc and Hemisfèric. The park has a lake where guests can hire rowboats, a kids' playground, and large open areas for outdoor activities like picnics.

5. Albufera Natural Park: This nearby park features wetlands, dunes, and a sizable freshwater lake in a natural environment. Birdwatchers and other nature lovers will find this natural reserve to be a refuge. Boat excursions on the lake allow visitors to experience Valencia's distinctive biological setting while taking in the city's breathtaking sunsets.

6. Central Park, also known as Parque Central, is one of Spain's largest urban parks and is now being constructed. It seeks to establish a green lung in the heart of the city, offering a refuge for enjoyment to both locals and visitors.

Albufera Natural Park Excursion

1. Albufera Natural Park is a vast wetland reserve with a diversified ecology made up of freshwater lakes, marshes, dunes, and rice fields. It is known as nature's oasis. As a result of its biological importance, it has been designated as a Ramsar site, recognizing its value as a migratory bird wetland of international significance.

2. Birdwatchers' Paradise: The park is a haven for avian species, making it a haven for birdwatchers. Keep your binoculars ready to spot the stunning birds that call Albufera home, including graceful herons, graceful egrets,

colorful kingfishers, and more. For individuals interested in receiving professional insights into the park's avian treasures, guided birding tours are offered.

3. Boat Trips on the Lake: A leisurely boat ride on the serene lake is one of the pleasures of an excursion to Albufera. Get on a traditional wooden boat, or "barca," and cruise around the tranquil waters while taking in the stunning scenery and peaceful solitude. The experience is simply magical as the sun sets over the horizon, creating a mesmerizing spectacle from the reflections on the sea.

4. Breathtaking Sunsets: Albufera is known for its magnificent sunsets, and the views from the lake are nothing short of amazing. The sky is painted in vibrant shades of orange, pink, and purple, which warmly illuminates the surrounding landscape. Awe-inspiring and

memorable is the sight of the sun descending below the horizon.

5. Gastronomic Delights: Albufera is not only a feast for the eyes, but it is also a culinary delight. The region is renowned for its rice fields and is the origin of the popular paella dish from Valencia. Enjoy a typical Valencian paella at one of the picturesque lakeside eateries after your boat ride. Enjoy the dish's genuine flavors, which frequently include fresh seafood gathered in the lake.

6. Environmental Education: Albufera Natural Park is dedicated to preserving the environment and spreading environmental awareness. The sensitive ecosystem of the park, sustainable practices, and the significance of maintaining this priceless natural asset for future generations are all topics that visitors can learn about.

Chapter Seven

Outdoor Adventures

Hiking and Trekking Routes

1. Calderona Natural Park: This park, which is immediately to the north of Valencia, has many hiking paths that snake through craggy mountains, lush forests, and historic ruins. The park's varied topography makes it appropriate for both easy strolls and strenuous treks.

2. Ruta de los Monasterios (Route of the Monasteries): The "Route of the Monasteries" is a historical path that leads you through history while passing by numerous medieval monasteries and cathedrals. The path winds past charming villages and gorgeous valleys, providing an intriguing look into the area's religious history.

3. Albufera Natural Park Trails: paths in the Albufera Natural Park: Albufera is famous for its wetlands and boat cruises, but it also has beautiful hiking paths that run alongside its lakes and marshes. The park is a wonderful location for those who love the outdoors because of its serene setting and diverse birds.

4. Montgó Natural Park: Located close to the seaside town of Dénia, Montgó Natural Park is home to a strenuous walk up Montgó Mountain. A stunning panoramic view of the shoreline and the surroundings will be your reward for your hard work.

5. Sierra de Espadán Natural Park: With its thick forests, rough peaks, and cool springs, the Sierra de Espadán Natural Park is a hiker's delight. It's a terrific place for families and lone adventurers alike because the well-marked routes appeal to varied abilities.

6. El Garb Peak: One of Valencia's most well-traveled trails leads to El Garb Peak, which is located in Sierra Calderona. The top is a great location for sunrise or sunset treks since it provides breathtaking views of the city and coastline.

7. The Turia Riverbed Gardens offer a green haven along the former riverbed for a stroll through the city. It's the ideal choice for a tranquil outdoor escape without leaving the city thanks to its many walking and cycling pathways, lush gardens, and open areas.

Before beginning your hiking excursion, make sure you have the right gear, enough water, and a map or GPS device. To ensure a safe and enjoyable journey, you should also check the weather forecast and take the trail's difficulty into account.

Water Sports and Activities

1. Windsurfing and kitesurfing: Valencia's beaches are ideal for windsurfing and kitesurfing because of consistent winds and great conditions. There are schools and rental businesses along the coast that accommodate all skill levels and offer tools and instruction to get you started or improve your abilities, whether you're a seasoned pro or a novice.

2. Sailing and yachting: The Mediterranean Sea's clear waters and pleasant climate entice sailors and yachting lovers. Explore the gorgeous coastline and adjacent islands by renting a sailboat or yacht. The marinas of Valencia, notably the Marina Real Juan Carlos I, provide amenities and services for sailors.

3. Jet skiing is an amazing way to feel the adrenaline rush of the sea. You may hire jet skis and go on guided tours in approved places on

Valencia's beaches, experiencing the rush of this fast-paced water sport.

4. Paddleboarding and kayaking are popular water sports for those seeking a more serene experience. For a distinctive view of Valencia's coastline, cruise the calm waters of Albufera Natural Park or head out to the Mediterranean.

5. Scuba Diving and Snorkelling: Take part in scuba diving or snorkeling to explore the thriving marine life under the waters. Underwater beauties abound in Valencia's waters, and diving outfitters provide guided tours to see these amazing dive locations.

6. Beach volleyball: For fans of beach volleyball, Valencia's sandy beaches make the ideal playing field. Take part in a pickup game or organize a friendly competition on the beach with your friends.

7. Parasailing: Try parasailing for an exhilarating activity that mixes thrills and breathtaking scenery. Enjoy a bird's-eye view of the city and the shoreline as you soar far above the water while being linked to a parachute.

8. Fishing: The Valencian shore is a great place for fishermen to pursue their passion. The Mediterranean waters provide a range of fish species to catch, whether you cast your line from the shore or go on a fishing charter.

Chapter Eighth

Food and Drinks

Restaurants

1. Paella Restaurants: Restaurants serving paella: Valencia is well-known for producing the traditional rice dish that is known as paella. The freshest ingredients are used to make authentic paella in many of the city's restaurants, and it is cooked to perfection on classic paella pans. For a taste of this Valencian favorite, head to the beachside restaurants and take in the sea air and delectable aromas.

2. Tapas Bars: Valencia has a thriving and welcoming tapas culture. Discover charming tapas bars serving a variety of tiny plates that are overflowing with flavor as you stroll through the city's winding alleyways.

The tapas experience is a lovely way to savor a variety of Spanish specialties in one sitting, from patatas bravas to jamón ibérico.

3. Mercado Central: Mercado Central is a haven for foodies, offering a wide selection of local goods, fresh meats, seafood, and veggies. You can indulge in seasonal treats inside the market's attractive cafes, which serve cuisine that is freshly prepared at the market.

4. Michelin-Starred Restaurants: For those looking for a fine dining experience, Valencia is home to several establishments with Michelin stars that highlight the innovation and culinary artistry of skilled chefs. These places push the limits of flavor and presentation while providing a singular culinary experience.

5. Fusion and International Cuisine: Valencia's culinary scene features a variety of eateries that provide fusion cuisine and other international flavors in addition to traditional Spanish fare.

These restaurants provide a variety of cuisine, from Asian fusion dishes to compositions with Mediterranean influences.

6. Chiringuitos: You may find chiringuitos (beach bars) serving casual dining with magnificent sea views all along the beaches. They provide cool beverages, grilled fish, and seaside favorites while fostering a relaxed atmosphere ideal for a leisurely supper by the water.

7. Horchaterías: Valencia is renowned for its energizing horchata, a traditional tiger nut beverage. Horchateras offer this refreshing beverage and delectable fartons, a sweet pastry ideal for dipping. To taste this Valencian delight, you must go to a horchatera.

Local cuisine

1. Paella: Indulging in Valencian cuisine's most well-known dish, paella, is a must for any study of the cuisine. Paella is a delectable one-pot marvel made with rice, saffron, and a range of ingredients like chicken, rabbit, fish, and vegetables that capture the spirit of Valencia.

2. Horchata: Made from tiger nuts and flavored with cinnamon and sugar, horchata is a classic, refreshing drink. The finest way to enjoy this creamy, sweet beverage is with fartons, which are long, fluffy pastries ideal for dipping.

3. Arroz al Horno is a traditional Valencian dish that is filling and tasty. Arroz al Horno is a hearty and filling baked rice dish made with tender pig ribs, morcilla (black pudding), and chickpeas.

4. All i Pebre: A typical fisherman's stew made with eel, potatoes, garlic, paprika, and olive oil, All I Pebre is from the Albufera region. This recipe highlights the plethora of fresh seafood that can be found in Valencia's waters.

5. Fideuà: A delicious seafood meal that captures the flavors of the Mediterranean, fideuà is similar to paella but made using short, thin noodles rather than rice. Usually, alioli, a garlic mayonnaise sauce, is served with it.

6. Espencat: This vivacious and colorful salad is made out of roasted red peppers, eggplants, and tomatoes and is topped with salt, garlic, and olive oil. This appetizer honors the local produce's freshness.

7. Oranges: Valencia is known for growing tasty oranges in its rich fields. For a zesty treat, sip on freshly squeezed orange juice or try delicacies like orange-flavored sponge cake.

8. Buñuelos: A popular sweet food, buuelos are fluffy, light fritters that are typically served during celebrations and special occasions. They can be eaten simply or stuffed with cream or chocolate and are frequently coated with powdered sugar.

Local Drinks

1. Horchata: Horchata is one of Valencia's most well-known and enduring beverages. Horchata is a creamy and cooling plant-based beverage that is made from chufa, commonly referred to as tiger nuts. It is a delicious blend of sweetness and nutty earthiness from cinnamon and sugar flavoring. Horchata is a popular alternative to relieve your thirst on hot summer days and is best consumed cold.

2. Agua de Valencia is a joyous and bubbly cocktail that honors Valencia's abundant citrus harvest. Orange juice, cava (Spanish sparkling

wine), vodka, and a dash of gin are all ingredients in Agua de Valencia. The outcome is a fizzy, fruity beverage that's great for celebrating milestones or just having a fun night with friends.

3. Mistela: In Valencian culture, mistela is revered as a classic sweet wine. Mistela is a fortified wine made from Moscatel or Malvasia grape juice that has a slight brandy flavor. This decadently sweet wine, which highlights the region's winemaking history, is frequently drunk as a digestif or coupled with pastries.

4. Cerveza Artesana: A rising number of regional breweries are creating artisanal beers in Valencia, which has embraced the craft beer movement. Valencia's craft beers, which range from IPAs to stouts, exhibit originality and excellent craftsmanship and provide beer fans with a wide variety of options to explore.

5. Café del Temps: Café del Temps, which translates to "Coffee of Time," is a distinctive local custom. It entails placing an order for a café with hielo (coffee with ice) and a side glass of Agua de Valencia. The aim is to gradually add the Agua de Valencia to your coffee while you slowly sip it while chatting with family and friends, providing a wonderful and leisurely experience.

6. Vermut: Made with rich fortified wine and fragrant herbs and spices, vermut is a specialty of Valencia. Vermut is frequently served over ice and topped with an orange or an olive when consumed as an aperitif. It creates the ideal atmosphere for a laid-back day of tapas and mingling.

Street Foods

1. Bocadillo de Calamares, sometimes known as a calamari sandwich, is one of Valencia's most popular street dishes. Crispy fried calamari rings are stuffed inside a warm baguette and frequently sprinkled with lemon or aioli for an additional flavor boost. It's a well-liked option for a quick and filling snack when traveling.

2. Churros con Chocolate: Churros con Chocolate is a traditional Spanish sweet that is a favorite indulgence. With a thick and decadent chocolate dipping sauce, these deep-fried dough pastries are offered with a crispy outside and soft interior. Churros con Chocolate is a delicious street dish that satisfies any sweet appetite, whether it is eaten for breakfast or as a midday pick-me-up.

3. Empanadas: In Valencia, you can find these tasty turnovers on many street corners. Empanadas are the ideal portable snack for a

speedy and savory nibble. They can be filled with a range of foods, such as meat, chicken, or veggies.

4. Buñuelos; The delectable fritters known as Buñuelos are fluffy and airy and coated with powdered sugar. These delicious delights are a favorite street food among both locals and visitors and are frequently savored during festivals and special occasions.

5. Pinchos: Similar to tapas, pinchos are little snacks that are typically served on a skewer or toothpick. The toppings can range from cured meats, cheese, and even shellfish to marinated olives. Pinchos are a terrific way to try several different flavors all at once.

6. Patatas Bravas: If you visit Valencia, you must sample this traditional Spanish street dish. Served with a fiery tomato-based sauce, garlic aioli, and crispy fried potatoes, this dish has a delectable medley of textures and tastes.

7. Döner Kebabs: The availability of döner kebabs, a well-liked street snack with Turkish cuisine origins, is a clear indication of Valencia's multicultural influence. Typically, seasoned beef slices are wrapped or served in a pita with fresh veggies and creamy sauces.

8. Roasted chestnuts are a cozy and enticing snack that warms hands and hearts that are sold by street vendors throughout the winter months.

Chapter Nine

Entertainment and Nightlife

Pubs and bars

1. Tapas Bars: Valencia's bar scene is heavily influenced by the tapas culture. Many pubs serve a broad variety of delectable tapas, from more contemporary and inventive small plates to traditional Spanish favorites like croquetas and patatas bravas. For a nice and relaxed dining experience, serve your tapas with a chilled beer or a delicious glass of local wine.

2. Cervecerías: Beer bars, or Cervecerías, are a favorite hangout for both locals and visitors. They offer a wide selection of beers, including both domestic and imported favorites as well as regional craft brewers. It's a terrific location for mingling, sipping cold beer, and trying out different kinds of beer.

3. Vermuterías: Valencians traditionally enjoy vermut, or vermouth, as an aperitif before dinner. Vermuterías specialize in serving several types of vermouth, frequently together with small nibbles or tapas. It's the ideal way to kick off a night of dining and socializing.

4. Coctelerías: Valencia's Coctelerías provide a refuge of mixology ingenuity for cocktail connoisseurs. With the use of premium spirits and seasonal ingredients, talented bartenders create creative and traditional cocktails that guarantee a great drinking experience.

5. Irish Pubs: Take in Valencia's lively and friendly environment in an Irish pub. These places provide a taste of Ireland by providing a large assortment of beers and spirits, live entertainment, and a pleasant atmosphere.

6. Music Bars: Valencia's music bars appeal to a variety of tastes by hosting themed music nights, DJ sets, and live performances. Dance

the night away to today's top tunes or sway to the beats of live jazz, rock, or flamenco ensembles.

7. Rooftop Bars: Rooftop bars in Valencia make the most of the gorgeous views that the city's coastal location has to offer. Take in the spectacular views of the city and the Mediterranean Sea while sipping on your favorite beverage.

8. Historic Taverns: Some of Valencia's pubs have a long, illustrious history. These charming and unique old pubs offer a window into the city's past while offering up customary libations and fare.

Clubs and Live Music Locations

1. Nightclubs: Valencia is home to a wide range of nightclubs that include various musical styles and ambiances. You may choose a nightclub to fit your taste, whether you prefer Latin beats, commercial songs, or electronic dance music.

Clubs frequently host themed events and parties that draw both locals and visitors looking for a fun-filled evening of dancing and mingling.

2. Live Music Venues: Valencia's live music venues are a must-visit for music lovers. These locations present a wide variety of acts, including rock, jazz, flamenco, and other genres, in settings ranging from small, cozy taverns to bigger concert halls. Discover the passion and skill of regional and international artists as they create a remarkable musical experience.

3. La Marina: The vibrant nightlife scene in the La Marina neighborhood is well-known. There are numerous taverns, clubs, and music venues in the vicinity, which contributes to the lively environment that lasts well into the morning. Both residents and tourists who want to go out on the town frequently visit this location.

4. Ruzafa: Another area of Valencia with thriving nightlife is Ruzafa. A variety of hip bars live music venues, and alternative clubs can be found here, all of which appeal to a more diverse and bohemian clientele.

5. Themed Parties & Events: Valencia is home to a large number of nightclubs and places where live music is performed. These occasions, which range from music festivals to costume parties, boost the excitement and fun factor of the nightlife.

6. Beach Clubs: Beach clubs have a special chance to flourish due to Valencia's seaside position. Beach clubs come alive in the warmer months, offering a mix of dancing, music, and relaxing by the water. Drink in the sounds of the DJ or live bands while relaxing with your feet in the sand.

7. Alternative Venues: Valencia is home to a variety of music venues that support independent, underground, and experimental music. These places give up-and-coming musicians and artists a stage, enhancing the nightlife scene with a dash of originality and innovation.

Chapter Ten

Safety and Health

Vaccinations

1. immunizations suggested by your native country: Make sure you are up to date on any prescribed immunizations. Measles, mumps, rubella (MMR), diphtheria, tetanus, pertussis (DTaP), polio, and influenza are among the immunizations that may be included in this list.

2. Hepatitis A: Contaminated food and water can spread the virus that causes hepatitis A. Before visiting Valencia, it is important to get vaccinated against Hepatitis A, especially if you intend to sample local street food or eat at more intimate restaurants.

3. Hepatitis B is a viral infection that can be passed from person to person by blood, intercourse, and contaminated needles.

If you'll be participating in activities that could put you in danger, such as medical procedures or close contact with locals, you should get vaccinated against Hepatitis B.

4. Typhoid: Contaminated food and water can lead to the bacterial infection typhoid. Consider obtaining a typhoid shot if you intend to eat at neighborhood eateries or food carts.

5. Although rabies is uncommon in Valencia, getting vaccinated against it is still a smart idea, especially if you plan to engage in outdoor activities or come into close contact with animals.

6. Check the most recent COVID-19 immunization requirements and travel restrictions for Valencia in light of the most recent travel advisories. Make sure you have got any mandatory COVID-19 vaccinations and that you own the proper entrance papers.

Discuss any extra vaccines or preventive measures based on your travel schedule and health status with a healthcare provider or travel medicine specialist before departure to determine your particular health needs.

Dealing with Emergencies

1. Make sure you are familiar with Valencia's emergency phone numbers. Police, medical, and fire emergencies can all be reported to 112, Spain's universal emergency number. You can also get in touch with the neighborhood police at 091 if you require specific assistance, such as reporting a crime.

2. Medical Emergencies: In the event of a medical emergency, phone 112 or go to the closest hospital or medical facility to get immediate assistance. You can be sure that you'll get the appropriate medical care because Valencia boasts first-rate medical facilities.

3. Language Barriers: Although English is widely spoken in Valencia, particularly in tourist areas, it is nevertheless advisable to acquire some fundamental Spanish words and phrases to communicate in an emergency. To get over language obstacles, having a translation software or phrasebook on hand might be helpful.

4. Make sure you have comprehensive travel insurance that covers medical emergencies, trip cancellations, and other unforeseen events before you leave on your vacation. Keep a copy of your insurance policy on hand, along with your contact information.

5. Items that Have Been Lost or Stolen: If the unlucky event occurs that you have lost or had items stolen, report the incident to the local authorities as soon as you can. Obtain a police record to support any required replacements or claims and for insurance purposes.

6. Natural disasters: Valencia is generally spared from natural calamities, but it's still a good idea to stay aware of the local weather and heed any instructions or warnings given by the authorities, particularly in the rare event of severe weather occurrences.

7. Consulate or Embassy: Be aware of the location and phone number of the consulate or embassy of your nation in Valencia. When there are serious emergencies, such as lost passports or legal problems, they can help.

8. Remain Calm: It's important to maintain your composure and calm in any emergency circumstance. Consider the circumstances, put your safety first, and ask for assistance if needed. Avoid taking unwarranted chances and heed the advice of local authorities.

9. Know Your Environment: Get to know the neighborhood you're staying in, especially where the closest hospital, police station, and embassy or consulate are located. Being aware of your surroundings will help you get through any emergency scenarios.

Conclusion

As we come to the end of the "**Valencia Travel Guide 2023-2024**," we hope that this journey has left you with cherished memories and a profound appreciation for the wonders of this captivating region. From the sun-kissed beaches that invite relaxation to the grandeur of historical landmarks and the tantalizing flavors of Valencian cuisine, Valencia has proven itself to be a destination that captures the heart and soul of every traveler.

In the year 2023-2024, we've witnessed Valencia come alive with festivals, cultural events, and sustainable initiatives that showcase its rich heritage and commitment to preserving its natural beauty. As you ventured through the historic center, explored art galleries, and mingled with the locals, you've undoubtedly experienced the warmth and authenticity that define this radiant coastal jewel.

Beyond the iconic sights, we hope you've also embraced the essence of Valencia - a place where tradition harmonizes with modernity, and history intertwines with innovation. Perhaps you've discovered your favorite nooks, savored flavors you've never imagined, or found solace in the tranquility of its parks and gardens. Each encounter with Valencia's culture and people has, we believe, left an indelible mark on your travel experience.

As you bid farewell to this enchanting city, we encourage you to carry the spirit of Valencia with you on your future adventures. May the vibrant colors of the Fallas festival linger in your memories, the rhythm of flamenco dance echo in your heart, and the taste of paella always bring a smile to your face.

Remember that travel is not just about the places we visit but the connections we make along the way. The friendships forged and the stories shared enrich our lives and broaden our perspectives. Valencia has welcomed you with open arms, and we hope you have felt the embrace of its unique charm.

In closing, we extend our heartfelt gratitude for choosing this guide as your companion on this exploration. We hope it has served you well, providing valuable insights and practical tips that made your trip to Valencia even more enjoyable.

As the pages of this book turn to a close, know that your journey doesn't have to end here. There are always more discoveries to be made, more experiences to be cherished, and more destinations to ignite your wanderlust.

From all of us who contributed to this guide, we wish you safe travels and an abundance of joy in your future adventures. May your path be filled with exploration, enlightenment, and a continuous thirst for the beauty that lies beyond the horizon.

Until we meet again, dear traveler, may the allure of Valencia stay with you as an ever-present reminder of the magic that awaits when you open your heart to the world.

Bon voyage and adiós from the "Valencia Travel Guide 2023-2024